ANNA SMITH

Ocean Full of Wonder

Text © Anna Smithers 2023

Illustrations © Nino Aptsiauri 2023

Book design by Victoria Smith

Orange Lotus Publishing

www.annasmithers.com

ISBN 978-1-8383391-6-6 - paperback

ISBN 978-1-8383391-9-7 - hardcover

For all the children of the world -

may the love of the ocean and nature show you the way

I'd like to introduce you to a very special friend.
It stretches on forever, and it doesn't seem to end.
In sun, it shines like precious jewels,
with gold and green and blue,
And if you listen closely, you can hear it humming too.

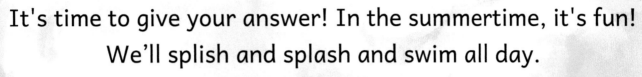

It's time to give your answer! In the summertime, it's fun!
We'll splish and splash and swim all day.
On toasty sand, we'll run.
Buried in its shallows, you can find all sorts of treasure.
We'll be **PIRATES** for a day
and hide them for good measure.

What's that you say? Yes – you're right!
The answer is the Ocean!
It's full of joy and wonder, amazing in its motion.
Beneath the ocean's surface, plants make oxygen for free,
To clean up harmful carbon from the bottom of the sea.

The ocean shapes the weather, and it keeps our planet warm,
By moving currents further north,
where sea life can **TRANSFORM**.
The ocean turns to clouds and then those clouds become the rain,
Which falls to Earth as precious water we can drink again.

The ocean gives us yummy food and routes for ships to sail.
Within it, you can surf, dive, fish or find an orca trail.
Although its parts have different names, it's one, without a doubt:
One single ocean, wide and deep, we **MUST** learn more about.

We'll find most coral reefs within a vibrant, tropic sea,
Protecting sandy coastlines from the currents and debris.
The structures, made from coral polyps, truly look sublime.
Inside them live their algae friends, who feed them all the time.

In chilly, shallow waters, we'll find forests green and vast,
with giant KELP and SEAGRASS,
which can grow extremely fast.
Those plants are quite remarkable and also very rare,
They soak up awful gases and they help us clean the air.

In the deep, open ocean, we'll chase dolphins in the sun.
We'll swim with turtles, cruise with sharks and have a lot of

FUN!

And if we're very lucky, we might meet a great blue whale –
They're longer than three buses, and they sing a dreamy tale.

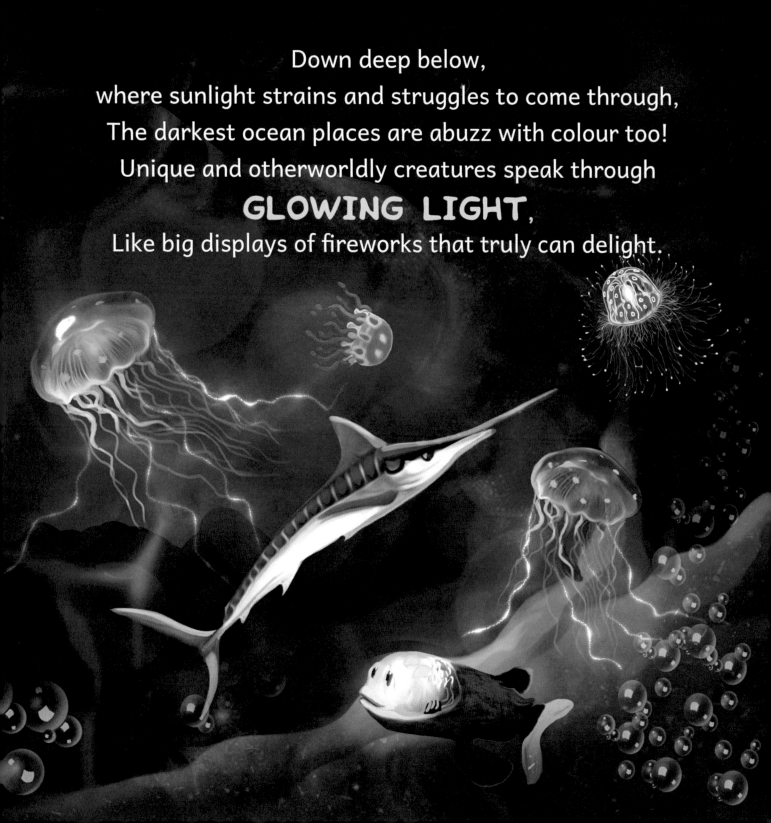

Down deep below,
where sunlight strains and struggles to come through,
The darkest ocean places are abuzz with colour too!
Unique and otherworldly creatures speak through
GLOWING LIGHT,
Like big displays of fireworks that truly can delight.

In recent years, the ocean has been under massive threat.
Warming seas and overfishing are problems we regret.

The worst of all is plastic waste, due to constant neglect.
Ocean creatures go extinct when their habitats are wrecked.

But there is hope!

We'll make a change with everything we do.
By saying "no" to plastic we'll protect the ocean too!
Compostable materials could make our ocean cleaner,
And litter picking on the beach will make the planet greener.

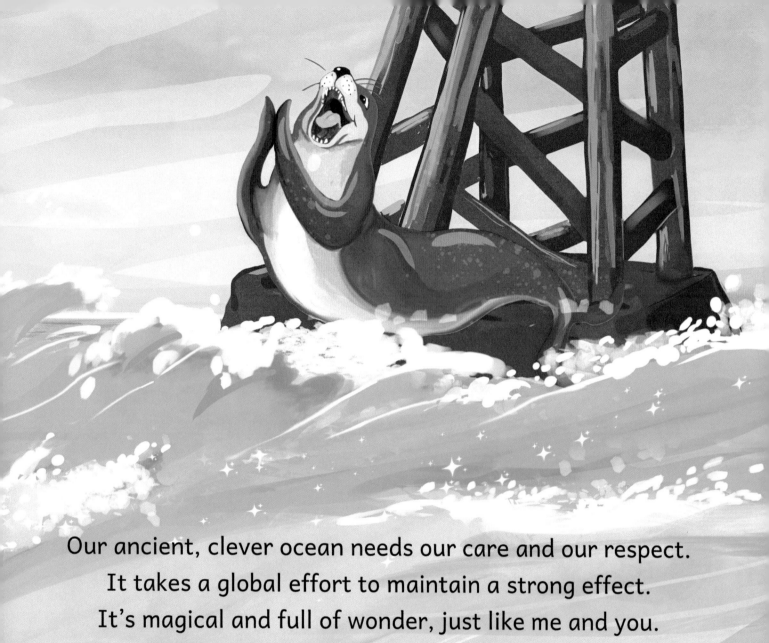

Our ancient, clever ocean needs our care and our respect.
It takes a global effort to maintain a strong effect.
It's magical and full of wonder, just like me and you.
It helped us through the ages, now we must

help it too!

Can you spot these sea creatures?

There are twelve sea creatures in this book.
Can you find and name them all?

 Starfish

 Sea lion

 Pyjama shark

 Octopus

 Sea turtle

 Dolphin

Crab

Orca

Sea otter

Seal

Swordfish

Blue whale

How can we help?

Our ocean is very, very old, it was created billions of years ago. And now it needs our help. What can we do every day?

1.  Use less plastic - Only 5-6% of plastic waste is recycled. Sometimes it takes up to 700 years for plastic to break down and most of it ends up in our ocean. We can help to make a difference by using more compostable materials and less 'single-use' plastic items. For example, we can use cotton or compostable bags when shopping, and reusable water bottles instead of buying single-use plastic ones. Can you think of other examples? Or maybe one day you'll invent cheap materials which are safe for the planet!

2.  Love and respect the ocean – Love the ocean, splash and swim in it, and go for a walk on the beach! Can you smell how different the air is? But remember that the ocean is also home to so many amazing creatures! From colourful fish to enormous whales, there is so much to love and respect. Fall in love with the ocean and nature, and you will become the 'Protector of the Ocean'!

3.  Keep the beaches clean - The beach is a fun place to play, swim and relax with family and friends, but we need to keep it clean and healthy for everyone to enjoy. When we leave rubbish on the beach, it can harm the environment and the creatures that live there. Let's always clean up after ourselves and put rubbish in the bins. That way, everyone can enjoy a fun and healthy day at the beach.

4.  Reduce harmful gases - Things like driving in cars and flying in aeroplanes create awful gases that the ocean soaks up. This is making the ocean warmer, which is destroying our coral reefs and sea creatures. We can make a difference though! By turning off lights and electronics when we're not using them. By walking, cycling, taking a train or a bus instead of driving. We can reuse and recycle, or try growing our own fruit and vegetables. These changes can help to keep our beautiful planet healthy for ourselves and future generations.

5.  Learn and share – Can you believe that we know less about the ocean than we know about space? There's still so much to discover! So read and watch everything that will help you to find out more about the beauty and wonder of the ocean. I love the "Blue Planet" series by Sir David Attenborough, it inspired me to write this book. Imagine what you can do! And then share your love with others and show them the beauty of our nature.

Other books by the author:

Dear adult – Thank you for reading this book. If you enjoyed it, please consider leaving a review. It would mean the world to me!

You can download your freebies here!

Hi children – I love receiving letters, drawings and pictures. Feel free to email anna@annasmithers.com and I will try my best to email you back!

A. Smithers

Made in the USA
Middletown, DE
08 September 2024

60643233R00020